Journal

BARBOUR
PUBLISHING

Consider the Lilies
ISBN 978-1-60260-886-3
Every Good Gift
ISBN 978-1-60260-887-0

Published by Barbour Publishing, Inc., P.O. box 719, Uhrichsville, OH 44683, www.barbourbooks.com

Our mission is to publish and distribute inspirational products offering exceptional value and biblical encouragement to the masses.

Printed in Thailand.

Come near to God and he
will come near to you.

James 4:8 NIV

"In the same way, let your light shine before men, that they may see your good deeds and praise your Father in heaven."
Matthew 5:-16 NIV

And be ye kind one to another, tenderhearted, forgiving one
another, even as God for Christ's sake hath forgiven you.
Ephesians 4:32 KJV

_____

_____

_____

_____

_____

_____

_____

_____

_____

_____

_____

_____

_____

_____

_____

_____

_____

_____

_____

_____

_____

_____

"By standing firm, you will win your souls."
Luke 2-1:-19 NLT

Providing for honest things, not only in the sight
of the Lord, but also in the sight of men.
2 Corinthians 8:21 KJV

For the Scriptures say, "If you want to enjoy life
and see many happy days, keep your tongue from
speaking evil and your lips from telling lies."
1 Peter 3:-10 NLT

Listen to counsel and accept discipline,
that you may be wise the rest of your days.
Proverbs 19:20 NASB

_____

_____

_____

_____

_____

_____

_____

_____

_____

_____

_____

_____

_____

_____

_____

_____

_____

_____

_____

_____

Dear brothers and sisters, when troubles come your way,
consider it an opportunity for great joy.

James 1:2 NLT

Do all things without grumbling or disputing.

Philippians 2:14 NASB

_____

_____

_____

_____

_____

_____

_____

_____

_____

_____

_____

_____

_____

_____

_____

_____

_____

_____

Thus speaketh the LORD of hosts, saying,
Execute true judgment, and shew mercy
and compassions every man to his brother.
Zechariah 7:9 KJV

When doubts filled my mind, your comfort
gave me renewed hope and cheer.
Psalm 94:-19 NLT

Be perfect, be of good comfort, be of one mind, live in peace;
and the God of love and peace shall be with you.

2 Corinthians 13:11 KJV

When words are many, sin is not absent,
but he who holds his tongue is wise.
Proverbs 10:19 NIV

Cast all your anxiety on him because he cares for you.
1 Peter 5:7 NIV

For our light affliction, which is but for a moment, worketh
for us a far more exceeding and eternal weight of glory.
2 Corinthians 4:-17 KJV

_____

_____

_____

_____

_____

_____

_____

_____

_____

_____

_____

_____

_____

_____

_____

_____

_____

_____

Be happy with those who are happy,
and weep with those who weep.
Romans 12:15 NLT

By this, love is perfected with us, so that we may have confidence in the day of judgment; because as He is, so also are we in this world.

-1 John 4:-17 NASB

Weeping may remain for a night,
but rejoicing comes in the morning.
Psalm 30:5 NIV

Thou wilt keep him in perfect peace, whose mind
is stayed on thee: because he trusteth in thee.

Isaiah 26:3 KJV

That ye be not slothful, but followers of them who
through faith and patience inherit the promises.
Hebrews 6:-12 KJV

Love wisdom like a sister; make insight
a beloved member of your family.

Proverbs 7:4 NLT

_____

_____

_____

_____

_____

_____

_____

_____

_____

_____

_____

_____

_____

_____

_____

_____

_____

_____

_____

_____

Dear friends, never take revenge. Leave that to
the righteous anger of God. For the Scriptures say,
"I will take revenge; I will pay them back," says the LORD.
Romans 12:19 NLT

Let your speech always be with grace,
as though seasoned with salt, so that you will
know how you should respond to each person.
Colossians 4:6 NASB

Every man shall give as he is able, according to the blessing
of the LORD thy God which he hath given thee.
Deuteronomy 16:17 KJV

The world is passing away, and also its lusts;
but the one who does the will of God lives forever.

1 John 2:17 NASB

Rejoicing in hope, persevering in
tribulation, devoted to prayer. . .
Romans 12:12 NASB

The LORD is close to the brokenhearted;
he rescues those whose spirits are crushed.
Psalm 34:-18 NLT

_____

_____

_____

_____

_____

_____

_____

_____

_____

_____

_____

_____

_____

_____

_____

_____

_____

_____

_____

_____

_____

A man has joy in an apt answer,
and how delightful is a timely word!
Proverbs 15:23 NASB

All discipline for the moment seems not to be joyful,
but sorrowful; yet to those who have been trained by it,
afterwards it yields the peaceful fruit of righteousness.

Hebrews 12:11 NASB

_____

_____

_____

_____

_____

_____

_____

_____

_____

_____

_____

_____

_____

_____

_____

_____

_____

_____

_____

_____

_____

_____

_____

_____

_____

_____

_____

_____

_____

_____

_____

_____

_____

_____

_____

_____

_____

_____

"But when you are praying, first forgive anyone
you are holding a grudge against, so that your
Father in heaven will forgive your sins, too."
Mark 11:25 NLT

"In everything, therefore, treat people the same way you want
them to treat you, for this is the Law and the Prophets."

Matthew 7:-12 NASB

_____

_____

_____

_____

_____

_____

_____

_____

_____

_____

_____

_____

_____

_____

_____

_____

_____

_____

_____

_____

_____

Oil and perfume make the heart glad,
so a man's counsel is sweet to his friend.
Proverbs 27:9 NASB

Jesus saith unto him, Thomas, because thou
hast seen me, thou hast believed: blessed are
they that have not seen, and yet have believed.

John 20:29 KJV

_____

_____

_____

_____

_____

_____

_____

_____

_____

_____

_____

_____

_____

_____

_____

_____

_____

_____

_____

For the Lord will be your confidence and
will keep your foot from being caught.
Proverbs 3:26 NASB

Instruct a wise man and he will be wiser still;
teach a righteous man and he will add to his learning.

Proverbs 9:9 NIV

_____

_____

_____

_____

_____

_____

_____

_____

_____

_____

_____

_____

_____

_____

_____

_____

_____

_____

Control your temper, for anger labels you a fool.
Ecclesiastes 7:9 NLT

"Look! I stand at the door and knock. If you hear my voice and open the door, I will come in, and we will share a meal together as friends."

Revelation 3:20 NLT

_____

_____

_____

_____

_____

_____

_____

_____

_____

_____

_____

_____

_____

_____

_____

_____

_____

_____

_____

_____

Rejoice in our confident hope.
Be patient in trouble, and keep on praying.

Romans 12:12 NLT

He answereth and saith unto them,
He that hath two coats,
let him impart to him that hath none;
and he that hath meat, let him do likewise.

Luke 3:-1-1 KJV

_____

_____

_____

_____

_____

_____

_____

_____

_____

_____

_____

_____

_____

_____

_____

_____

_____

_____

_____

_____

_____

Turn from evil and do good;
seek peace and pursue it.
Psalm 34:14 NIV

Pray for us, for we are sure that we have a good conscience,
desiring to conduct ourselves honorably in all things.

Hebrews 13:-18 NASB

_____

_____

_____

_____

_____

_____

_____

_____

_____

_____

_____

_____

_____

_____

_____

_____

_____

_____

_____

_____

_____

A hard worker has plenty of food,
but a person who chases fantasies has no sense.
Proverbs 12:11 NLT

He will judge the world with justice
and rule the nations with fairness.

Psalm 9:8 NLT

Starting a quarrel is like breaching a dam;
so drop the matter before a dispute breaks out.
Proverbs 17:14 NIV

Serve the LORD with gladness:
come before his presence with singing.

Psalm 100:2 KJV

_____

_____

_____

_____

_____

_____

_____

_____

_____

_____

_____

_____

_____

_____

_____

_____

_____

_____

_____

_____

_____

_____

_____

_____

_____

_____

_____

_____

_____

_____

_____

_____

_____

_____

_____

_____

_____

_____

_____

"Do not judge, and you will not be judged.
Do not condemn, and you will not be condemned.
Forgive, and you will be forgiven."
Luke 6:37 NIV

Make a joyful noise unto God,
all ye lands.
Psalm 66:1 KJV

How much better is it to get wisdom than gold!
and to get understanding rather to be chosen than silver!
Proverbs 16:16 KJV

For the LORD your God will bless you in all your harvest and in all the work of your hands, and your joy will be complete.

Deuteronomy 16:15 NIV

_____

_____

_____

_____

_____

_____

_____

_____

_____

_____

_____

_____

_____

_____

_____

_____

_____

_____

_____

A cheerful heart is good medicine.
Proverbs 17:22 NIV

But the Holy Spirit produces this kind of fruit in our lives:
love, joy, peace, patience, kindness, goodness, faithfulness.

Galatians 5:22 NLT

_____

_____

_____

_____

_____

_____

_____

_____

_____

_____

_____

_____

_____

_____

_____

_____

_____

_____

_____

And herein do I exercise myself, to have always a conscience void of offence toward God, and toward men.

Acts 24:16 KJV

Consider the blameless, observe the upright;
there is a future for the man of peace.

Psalm 37:37 NIV

_____

_____

_____

_____

_____

_____

_____

_____

_____

_____

_____

_____

_____

_____

_____

_____

_____

_____

_____

There will always be poor people in the land. Therefore
I command you to be openhanded toward your brothers
and toward the poor and needy in your land.

Deuteronomy 15:11 NIV

People with understanding control their anger;
a hot temper shows great foolishness.

Proverbs 14:29 NLT

_____

_____

_____

_____

_____

_____

_____

_____

_____

_____

_____

_____

_____

_____

_____

_____

_____

_____

_____

_____

_____

_____

_____

_____

_____

_____

_____

_____

_____

_____

_____

_____

_____

_____

_____

_____

_____

_____

_____

_____

_____

_____

Relax, everything's going to be all right; rest, everything's coming together; open your hearts, love is on the way!
Jude 1:2 MSG

But the wisdom that is from above is first pure, then peaceable, gentle, and easy to be intreated, full of mercy and good fruits, without partiality, and without hypocrisy.

James 3:-17 KJV

_____

_____

_____

_____

_____

_____

_____

_____

_____

_____

_____

_____

_____

_____

_____

_____

_____

_____

Your word is a lamp to my feet
and a light for my path.
Psalm 119:105 NIV

These things, which ye have both learned,
and received, and heard, and seen in me, do:
and the God of peace shall be with you.

Philippians 4:9 KJV

_____

_____

_____

_____

_____

_____

_____

_____

_____

_____

_____

_____

_____

_____

_____

_____

_____

_____

_____

_____

_____

_____

_____

_____

_____

_____

_____

_____

_____

_____

_____

_____

_____

_____

_____

_____

_____

_____

_____

_____

_____

He who guards his mouth and his
tongue keeps himself from calamity.
Proverbs 21:23 NIV

Those who plant in tears will harvest with shouts of joy.
They weep as they go to plant their seed,
but they sing as they return with the harvest.

Psalm 126:5–6 NLT

_____

_____

_____

_____

_____

_____

_____

_____

_____

_____

_____

_____

_____

_____

_____

_____

_____

"They will fight against you, but they will not overcome you,
for I am with you to deliver you," declares the LORD.
Jeremiah 1:19 NASB

For every creature of God is good, and nothing to
be refused, if it be received with thanksgiving.
1 Timothy 4:4 KJV

_____

_____

_____

_____

_____

_____

_____

_____

_____

_____

_____

_____

_____

_____

_____

_____

_____

_____

_____

I will both lay me down in peace, and sleep:
for thou, LORD, only makest me dwell in safety.
Psalm 4:8 KJV

Be of the same mind one toward another. . . .
Recompense to no man evil for evil.
Provide things honest in the sight of all men.
Romans 12:16—17 KJV

_____

_____

_____

_____

_____

_____

_____

_____

_____

_____

_____

_____

_____

_____

_____

_____

_____

_____

Each man should give what he has decided in his heart to give, not reluctantly or under compulsion, for God loves a cheerful giver.

2 Corinthians 9:7 NIV

Always be humble and gentle. Be patient with each other, making allowance for each other's faults because of your love.

Ephesians 4:2 NLT

He has removed our sins as far from
us as the east is from the west.
Psalm 103:12 NLT

For God's gifts and his call
can never be withdrawn.
Romans 11:29 NLT

Blessed are the meek; for they shall inherit the earth.
Matthew 5:5 KJV

Without consultation, plans are frustrated,
but with many counselors they succeed.
Proverbs 15:22 NASB

_____

_____

_____

_____

_____

_____

_____

_____

_____

_____

_____

_____

_____

_____

_____

_____

_____

_____

_____

_____

_____

_____

_____

_____

_____

_____

_____

_____

_____

_____

_____

_____

_____

_____

_____

_____

_____

_____

Be of good courage, and he shall strengthen your heart,
all ye that hope in the LORD.
Psalm 31:24 KJV

"He cuts off every branch in me that bears no fruit,
while every branch that does bear fruit he prunes
so that it will be even more fruitful."

John 15:2 NIV

_____

_____

_____

_____

_____

_____

_____

_____

_____

_____

_____

_____

_____

_____

_____

_____

_____

_____

_____

"I will always show you where to go."
Isaiah 58:11 MSG

O Lord, You have heard the prayers of those
who have no pride. You will give strength
to their heart, and You will listen to them.
Psalm 10:17 NLV

_____

_____

_____

_____

_____

_____

_____

_____

_____

_____

_____

_____

_____

_____

_____

_____

_____

Great is the LORD, and highly to be praised, and His greatness is unsearchable. One generation shall praise Your works to another, and shall declare Your mighty acts.
Psalm 145:3–4 NASB

Therefore encourage one another and build
up one another, just as you also are doing.
1 Thessalonians 5:-1-1 NASB

Be thou faithful unto death, and I
will give thee a crown of life.
Revelation 2:10 KJV

And this is the promise that he hath
promised us, even eternal life.

1 John 2:25 KJV

Beyond all these things put on love,
which is the perfect bond of unity.
Colossians 3:-14 *NASB*

"I will give to each one of you
according to your deeds."
Revelation 2:23 NASB

_____

_____

_____

_____

_____

_____

_____

_____

_____

_____

_____

_____

_____

_____

_____

_____

_____

_____

_____

_____

_____

_____

He who conceals his transgressions will not prosper, but he who confesses and forsakes them will find compassion.
Proverbs 28:-13 NASB

I will rejoice in the Lord, I will
joy in the God of my salvation.
Habakkuk 3:-18 KJV

_____

_____

_____

_____

_____

_____

_____

_____

_____

_____

_____

_____

_____

_____

_____

_____

_____

_____

_____

Be kindly affectioned one to another with brotherly love;
in honour preferring one another.

Romans 12:10 KJV

He who trusts in his riches will fall, but those who
are right with God will grow like a green leaf.
Proverbs 11:28 NLV

_____

_____

_____

_____

_____

_____

_____

_____

_____

_____

_____

_____

_____

_____

_____

_____

_____

_____

_____

_____

Be to me a rock of habitation to which I may
continually come; You have given commandment
to save me, for You are my rock and my fortress.
Psalm 71:3 NASB

Let us then approach the throne of grace
with confidence, so that we may receive mercy
and find grace to help us in our time of need.

Hebrews 4:-16 NIV

"It will also come to pass that before they call, I will answer; and while they are still speaking, I will hear."
Isaiah 65:24 NASB

The testing of your faith produces endurance. And let
endurance have its perfect result, so that you may
be perfect and complete, lacking in nothing.

James 1:3–4 NASB

For God has given wisdom and much learning
and joy to the person who is good in God's eyes.
Ecclesiastes 2:26 NLV

Now then we are ambassadors for Christ.
2 Corinthians 5:20 KJV

Cast thy burden upon the Lord, and he shall sustain thee:
he shall never suffer the righteous to be moved.
Psalm 55:22 KJV

These hard times are small potatoes compared to the coming
good times, the lavish celebration prepared for us.

2 Corinthians 4:17 MSG

All the paths of the LORD are mercy and truth unto
such as keep his covenant and his testimonies.
Psalm 25:-10 KJV

"Be on your guard! If your brother sins, rebuke him;
and if he repents, forgive him."
Luke 17:3 NASB

_____

_____

_____

_____

_____

_____

_____

_____

_____

_____

_____

_____

_____

_____

_____

_____

_____

_____

_____

Wisdom reposes in the heart of the discerning
and even among fools she lets herself be known.

Proverbs 14:33 NIV

Owe nothing to anyone except to love one another;
for he who loves his neighbor has fulfilled the law.

Romans 13:8 NASB

For God hath not given us the spirit of fear;
but of power, and of love, and of a sound mind.
2 Timothy 1:7 KJV

Iron sharpeneth iron; so a man sharpeneth
the countenance of his friend.
Proverbs 27:-17 KJV

Be of the same mind toward one another;
do not be haughty in mind, but associate with the lowly.
Do not be wise in your own estimation.

Romans 12:16 NASB

Thou knowest my downsitting and mine uprising,
thou understandest my thought afar off.
Psalm 139:2 KJV

Blessed are the pure in heart; for they shall see God.
Matthew 5:8 KJV

"I am the door; if anyone enters through Me, he will be saved, and will go in and out and find pasture."
John 10:9 NASB

_____

_____

_____

_____

_____

_____

_____

_____

_____

_____

_____

_____

_____

_____

_____

_____

_____

_____

_____

_____

So then we pursue the things which make
for peace and the building up of one another.
Romans 14:19 NASB

If a man therefore purge himself from these, he shall
be a vessel unto honour, sanctified, and meet for the
master's use, and prepared unto every good work.
2 Timothy 2:21 KJV

_____

_____

_____

_____

_____

_____

_____

_____

_____

_____

_____

_____

_____

_____

_____

_____

_____

_____

He mocks proud mockers
but gives grace to the humble.
Proverbs 3:34 NIV

One hand full of rest is better than two hands
full of work and trying to catch the wind.
Ecclesiastes 4:6 NLV

_____

_____

_____

_____

_____

_____

_____

_____

_____

_____

_____

_____

_____

_____

_____

_____

_____

_____

_____

_____

_____

Is anyone among you suffering? Then he must pray.
Is anyone cheerful? He is to sing praises.
James 5:-13 NASB

Use your whole body as an instrument
to do what is right for the glory of God.
Romans 6:-13 NLT

_____

_____

_____

_____

_____

_____

_____

_____

_____

_____

_____

_____

_____

_____

_____

_____

_____

_____

To the Lord our God belong mercies and forgiveness.
Daniel 9:9 KJV

For God did not give us a spirit of timidity,
but a spirit of power, of love and of self-discipline.

2 Timothy 1:7 NIV

_____

_____

_____

_____

_____

_____

_____

_____

_____

_____

_____

_____

_____

_____

_____

_____

_____

_____

_____

_____

Prove all things; hold fast that which is good.
1 Thessalonians 5:21 KJV

Thank you for making me so wonderfully complex!
Your workmanship is marvelous—how well I know it.
Psalm 139:14 NLT

_____

_____

_____

_____

_____

_____

_____

_____

_____

_____

_____

_____

_____

_____

_____

_____

_____

_____

_____

Whatever happens, conduct yourselves in
a manner worthy of the gospel of Christ.

Philippians 1:27 NIV

The lowly will possess the land and
will live in peace and prosperity.
Psalm 37:-1-1 NLT

_____

_____

_____

_____

_____

_____

_____

_____

_____

_____

_____

_____

_____

_____

_____

_____

_____

_____

_____

_____

_____

_____

_____

_____

_____

_____

_____

_____

_____

_____

_____

_____

_____

_____

_____

_____

_____

_____

_____

_____

_____

Do you see a man skilled in his work? He will stand
before kings; he will not stand before obscure men.
Proverbs 22:29 NASB

Stand fast therefore in the liberty wherewith Christ hath made us free, and be not entangled again with the yoke of bondage.

Galatians 5:-1 KJV

_____

_____

_____

_____

_____

_____

_____

_____

_____

_____

_____

_____

_____

_____

_____

_____

_____

_____

The wise woman builds her house,
but the foolish tears it down with her own hands.
Proverbs 14:1 NASB

Rejoicing in hope; patient in tribulation;
continuing instant in prayer.

Romans 12:12 KJV

"Now that you know these things,
you will be blessed if you do them."
John 13:17 NIV

The LORD liveth; and blessed be my rock; and
exalted be the God of the rock of my salvation.

2 Samuel 22:47 NLT

_____

_____

_____

_____

_____

_____

_____

_____

_____

_____

_____

_____

_____

_____

_____

_____

_____

_____

_____

"He will yet fill your mouth with laughter
and your lips with shouts of joy."
Job 8:2-1 NIV

"Learn to do good; seek justice, reprove the ruthless,
defend the orphan, plead for the widow."
Isaiah 1:17 NASB

_____

_____

_____

_____

_____

_____

_____

_____

_____

_____

_____

_____

_____

_____

_____

_____

_____

_____

_____

_____

_____

_____

_____

_____

_____

_____

_____

_____

_____

_____

_____

_____

_____

_____

_____

_____

_____

_____

GOD made everything with
a place and purpose.
Proverbs 16:4 MSG

Don't act thoughtlessly, but understand
what the Lord wants you to do.
Ephesians 5:-17 NLT

_____

_____

_____

_____

_____

_____

_____

_____

_____

_____

_____

_____

_____

_____

_____

_____

_____

_____

_____

_____

Tune me in to foot-tapping songs,
set these once-broken bones to dancing.
Psalm 5-1:8 MSG

So we must listen very carefully to the truth
we have heard, or we may drift away from it.
Hebrews 2:-1 NLT

_____

_____

_____

_____

_____

_____

_____

_____

_____

_____

_____

_____

_____

_____

_____

_____

_____

_____

The entrance of thy words giveth light;
it giveth understanding unto the simple.
Psalm 119:130 KJV

Since everything here today might well be gone tomorrow,
do you see how essential it is to live a holy life?
2 Peter 3:-1-1 MSG

_____

_____

_____

_____

_____

_____

_____

_____

_____

_____

_____

_____

_____

_____

_____

_____

_____

_____

_____

_____

Greater is he that is in you, than he that is in the world.
1 John 4:4 KJV

Is any among you afflicted? let him pray.
Is any merry? let him sing psalms.

James 5:-13 KJV

_____

_____

_____

_____

_____

_____

_____

_____

_____

_____

_____

_____

_____

_____

_____

_____

_____

_____

_____

_____

He satisfieth the longing soul,
and filleth the hungry soul with goodness.
Psalm 107:9 KJV

A heart that has peace is life to the body.
Proverbs 14:30 NLV

A merry heart doeth good like a medicine.
Proverbs 17:22 KJV

That doesn't mean you should all look and speak
and act the same. Out of the generosity of Christ,
each of us is given his own gift.

Ephesians 4:7 MSG

_____

_____

_____

_____

_____

_____

_____

_____

_____

_____

_____

_____

_____

_____

_____

_____

_____

I remember the days of old; I meditate on all thy works;
I muse on the work of thy hands.

Psalm 143:5 KJV

He has granted to us His precious and magnificent
promises, so that by them you may become
partakers of the divine nature.
2 Peter 1:4 NASB

_____

_____

_____

_____

_____

_____

_____

_____

_____

_____

_____

_____

_____

_____

_____

_____

_____

_____

_____

_____

_____

_____

_____

_____

_____

_____

_____

_____

_____

_____

_____

_____

_____

_____

_____

_____

_____

_____

If God be for us, who can be against us?
Romans 8:31 KJV

I know whom I have believed, and am persuaded
that he is able to keep that which I have committed
unto him against that day.

2 Timothy 1:-12 KJV

God's love is meteoric, his loyalty astronomic,
his purpose titanic, his verdicts oceanic.
Yet in his largeness nothing gets lost.
Psalm 36:5–6 MSG

Let us hold unswervingly to the hope we
profess, for he who promised is faithful.
Hebrews 10:23 NIV

Fear not, O land; be glad and rejoice:
for the LORD will do great things.
Joel 2:21 KJV

If you are angry, do not let it become sin.
Get over your anger before the day is finished.
Ephesians 4:26 NLV

_____

_____

_____

_____

_____

_____

_____

_____

_____

_____

_____

_____

_____

_____

_____

_____

_____

_____

"So be careful to keep the words of this agreement
and obey them so all that you do will go well."
Deuteronomy 29:9 NLV

The LORD will fulfill his purpose for me.
Psalm 138:8 NIV

_____

_____

_____

_____

_____

_____

_____

_____

_____

_____

_____

_____

_____

_____

_____

_____

_____

We glory in tribulations also: knowing that tribulation worketh
patience; and patience, experience; and experience, hope.
Romans 5:3—4 KJV

Whatsoever thy hand findeth to do, do it with thy might;
for there is no work, nor device, nor knowledge,
nor wisdom, in the grave, whither thou goest.

Ecclesiastes 9:-10 KJV

Beloved, let us love one another:
for love is of God; and every one that
loveth is born of God, and knoweth God.
-1 John 4:7 KJV

And so, having patiently waited,
he obtained the promise.
Hebrews 6:-15 NASB

_____

_____

_____

_____

_____

_____

_____

_____

_____

_____

_____

_____

_____

_____

_____

_____

_____

_____

_____

_____

Though an army besiege me, my heart will not fear; though war break out against me, even then will I be confident.
Psalm 27:3 NIV

The LORD is good unto them that wait
for him, to the soul that seeketh him.
Lamentations 3:25 KJV

It shall come to pass, that before they call, I will answer;
and while they are yet speaking, I will hear.

Isaiah 65:24 KJV

"The earth and everything
in it belongs to the Lord."
1 Corinthians 10:26 NLV

_____

_____

_____

_____

_____

_____

_____

_____

_____

_____

_____

_____

_____

_____

_____

_____

_____

_____

_____

_____

_____

If you do not have wisdom, ask God for it. He is always ready to give it to you and will never say you are wrong for asking.
James 1:5 NLV

If we are faithless, he will remain faithful,
for he cannot disown himself.

2 Timothy 2:-13 NIV

_____

_____

_____

_____

_____

_____

_____

_____

_____

_____

_____

_____

_____

_____

_____

_____

_____

_____

Christ in you brings hope of all the great things to come.
Colossians 1:27 NLV

Your ears will hear a word behind you, saying, "This is the way, walk in it," whenever you turn to the right or to the left.

Isaiah 30:21 NLV

_____

_____

_____

_____

_____

_____

_____

_____

_____

_____

_____

_____

_____

_____

_____

_____

_____

_____

_____

_____

_____

_____

_____

_____

_____

_____

_____

_____

_____

_____

_____

_____

_____

_____

_____

_____

_____

_____

God is our refuge and strength,
a very present help in trouble.
Psalm 46:-1 KJV

It is by faith you stand firm.
2 Corinthians 1:24 NIV

_____

_____

_____

_____

_____

_____

_____

_____

_____

_____

_____

_____

_____

_____

_____

_____

_____

_____

_____

_____

_____

_____

_____

_____

_____

_____

_____

_____

_____

_____

_____

_____

_____

_____

_____

_____

_____

_____

_____

_____

_____

"My Presence will go with you, and I will give you rest."
Exodus 33:-14 NIV

God sets the lonely in families, he leads forth the prisoners
with singing; but the rebellious live in a sun-scorched land.
Psalm 68:6 NIV

_____

_____

_____

_____

_____

_____

_____

_____

_____

_____

_____

_____

_____

_____

_____

_____

_____

_____

_____

"Even if you are driven to the ends of the earth, the Lord your God will gather you and bring you back."
Deuteronomy 30:4 NLV

"You are sad now. I will see you again and then your hearts will be full of joy. No one can take your joy from you."

John 16:22 NLV

_____

_____

_____

_____

_____

_____

_____

_____

_____

_____

_____

_____

_____

_____

_____

_____

_____

_____

_____

_____

_____

_____

_____

_____

_____

_____

_____

_____

_____

_____

_____

_____

_____

_____

_____

_____

_____

_____

_____

_____

_____

"Be sure of this: I am with you always,
even to the end of the age."
Matthew 28:20 NLT

GOD is gracious—it is he who makes things right,
our most compassionate God.
Psalm 116:5 MSG

_____

_____

_____

_____

_____

_____

_____

_____

_____

_____

_____

_____

_____

_____

_____

_____

_____

_____

_____

There is that speaketh like the piercings of a sword:
but the tongue of the wise is health.

Proverbs 12:18 KJV

Who will hurt you if you do what is right?
1 Peter 3:-13 NLV

_____

_____

_____

_____

_____

_____

_____

_____

_____

_____

_____

_____

_____

_____

_____

_____

_____

_____

_____

_____

_____

_____

_____

_____

_____

_____

_____

_____

_____

_____

_____

_____

_____

_____

_____

_____

_____

_____

In thy presence is fulness of joy;
at thy right hand there are pleasures for evermore.
Psalm 16:11 KJV

"The person who thinks he is important will find out how little he is worth. The person who is not trying to honor himself will be made important."

Matthew 23:-12 NLV

_____

_____

_____

_____

_____

_____

_____

_____

_____

_____

_____

_____

_____

_____

_____

_____

_____

_____

_____

Not slothful in business; fervent in spirit;
serving the Lord.
Romans 12:11 KJV

"Be strong and courageous, do not be afraid or tremble,
for the LORD your God is the one who goes with you.
He will not fail you or forsake you."
Deuteronomy 3-1:6 NASB

"The joy of the LORD is your strength."
Nehemiah 8:-10 NIV

Delight yourself in the LORD and he will
give you the desires of your heart.
Psalm 37:4 NIV

"I will refresh the weary and satisfy the faint."
Jeremiah 31:25 NIV

_____

_____

_____

_____

_____

_____

_____

_____

_____

_____

_____

_____

_____

_____

_____

_____

_____

_____

_____

_____

_____

Yea, happy is that people, whose God is the LORD.
Psalm 144:15 KJV

"Even the Son of Man came not to be served but to serve others and to give his life as a ransom for many."
Matthew 20:28 NLT

_____

_____

_____

_____

_____

_____

_____

_____

_____

_____

_____

_____

_____

_____

_____

_____

_____

_____

_____

What a God! His road stretches straight and smooth.
Every God-direction is road-tested. Everyone who
runs toward him makes it. Is there any god like God?

Psalm 18:30–31 MSG

It is well with the man who is gracious and lends;
he will maintain his cause in judgment.
Psalm 112:5 NASB

_____

_____

_____

_____

_____

_____

_____

_____

_____

_____

_____

_____

_____

_____

_____

_____

_____

_____

_____

Blessed are they which do hunger and thirst after
righteousness: for they shall be filled.
Matthew 5:6 KJV

He who loves a pure heart and whose speech
is gracious will have the king for his friend.
Proverbs 22:11 NIV

You must be willing to wait without giving up.
After you have done what God wants you to do,
God will give you what He promised you.
Hebrews 10:36 NLV

No one has ever seen God. But if we love each other, God lives in us, and his love is brought to full expression in us.

1 John 4:-12 NLT

Fight the good fight of faith; take hold of the eternal
life to which you were called, and you made the good
confession in the presence of many witnesses.

1 Timothy 6:12 NASB

A young man makes himself known by his actions
and proves if his ways are pure and right.
Proverbs 20:-11 NLV

I wait for the LORD, my soul doth wait,
and in his word do I hope.

Psalm 130:5 KJV

God has given us different gifts
for doing certain things well.

Romans 12:6 NLT

_____

_____

_____

_____

_____

_____

_____

_____

_____

_____

_____

_____

_____

_____

_____

_____

_____

_____

_____

Let them praise his name with dancing and
make music to him with tambourine and harp.
Psalm 149:3 NIV

Many are the plans in a man's heart,
but it is the LORD's purpose that prevails.
Proverbs 19:21 NIV

_____

_____

_____

_____

_____

_____

_____

_____

_____

_____

_____

_____

_____

_____

_____

_____

_____

Let patience have her perfect work, that ye
may be perfect and entire, wanting nothing.
James 1:4 KJV